Original title:
Christmas Bells and Winter Hues

Copyright © 2024 Creative Arts Management OÜ
All rights reserved.

Author: Franklin Stone
ISBN HARDBACK: 978-9916-94-108-9
ISBN PAPERBACK: 978-9916-94-109-6

Tinsel Trails and Fragrant Pines

In a forest of glitter, the squirrels all sing,
Dancing with ornaments, a whimsical fling.
One squirrel stole tinsel, shiny and bright,
Now he's wrapped in it, what a comical sight!

With pinecones for hats, they prance and they play,
A snowball soon launched—what a humorous fray!
The rabbits all chuckle and roll in the snow,
As twinkling lights flicker, putting on quite a show.

Radiant Sights of Holiday Cheer

The snowmen are grinning, with noses so large,
One tripped on a carrot; his friends took charge.
They rolled him in snow while the kids all declared,
"A snow fight's afoot! Just be suitably scared!"

With mittens and scarves, they're all decked out right,
But boots keep on squeaking—is something afoot?
The cocoa's all spilling, hot as the sun,
"Please don't spill it here!" they all shout out in fun.

A Winter's Embrace

The icicles glisten like teeth from a grin,
While penguins in flippers do a wild spin.
They slid on the ice, oh what a mad race,
Flapping and flailing, in an awkward embrace!

In knitwear galore, the old folks delight,
But one lady tripped, her wig took a flight.
The dog caught it mid-air and donned it with pride,
Now there's laughter and howling from each side.

Bright Echoes of the Past

Eggnog's the drink, with a hint of a cheer,
But Uncle Joe's got some stuck in his beard.
He tries to sip slowly, but spills on his pants,
Leaving us rolling, we can't take a chance!

The carolers' voices soar high and away,
They trip over snowdrifts in a jolly ballet.
With harmonies soaring, off key they resound,
Yet we all sing along, joyfully spellbound.

The Soft Tinkling of Frozen Moments

Frosty friends do shimmy and slide,
On an ice rink where squirrels abide.
Snowmen caper with carrot noses,
Chasing penguins who wear old poses.

Hot cocoa spills on mittens bright,
Laughter bubbles under twinkling light.
The cat in a scarf, oh what a sight,
With snowflakes landing on him just right.

Nightfall's Embrace in Shimmering Hues

The moon wears a hat, quite fancy indeed,
While snowflakes dance with unbridled speed.
Elves on rooftops check their lists twice,
Dreaming of treats that are ever so nice.

A raccoon slips, with a holiday cheer,
Into the stash of our best ginger beer.
Red-nosed reindeer would surely agree,
That this night of mischief is filled with glee.

Echoes of Wonder Beneath the Snowfall

A snowball fight erupts with great glee,
As neighbors dive for cover, wild and free.
Sleds race down hills, a slippery ride,
With laughter and giggles, we all collide.

The stockings hang low, full of surprise,
Oh look! A pair of bright, dancing ties.
As everyone chuckles, they can't help but see,
That the holiday spirit is timeless and free.

Shimmering Echoes of Joyous Evenings

With twinkling lights on every street,
The dog in a sweater thinks he's quite neat.
Gingerbread houses, a sweet little mess,
We giggle as frosting turns into stress.

Sipping cider as carolers croon,
A cat in a hat serenades the moon.
Jokes are exchanged, with a wink and a grin,
As we dance in our socks, let the fun begin!

Enchanted Whispers of the Arctic Night

In a frosty land where snowballs fly,
Santa's got a sleigh, but does he cry?
The reindeer chuckle, they're up to no good,
While elves throw snowmen, dressed up as they should.

Under twinkling stars, hot cocoa spills,
With marshmallow hats, oh what a thrill!
Snowflakes dance like they're in ballet,
While penguins slide down, singing hooray!

Adorned with the Essence of Fire and Ice

A snowman wearing shades, looking quite cool,
With a carrot-nose grin, breaking all the rules.
The fireplace flickers, with stories so grand,
Of llamas on sleds, gliding o'er the land.

Gingerbread houses, they smell divine,
But the mice are baking? Oh, that's just fine!
A pie in the window, so tempting and round,
But watch out! It's flying, just hit the ground!

Frosted Memories in the Glow of Evenings

Check out the cat, with tinsel on its tail,
Chasing the shadows, it's off like a whale.
The fireplace chuckles, with embers so bright,
"Rudolph's in trouble; he can't fly tonight!"

The snowflakes giggle as they softly land,
While squirrels play poker with acorns in hand.
With cocoa in mugs, and laughter so bold,
The warmth of togetherness is joy to behold.

Comfort in the Embrace of Winter Light

When icicles glitter, they look like a crown,
Sipping on warm drinks, we laugh and we frown.
The power went out, but we'll make it work,
With candles and shadows, we dance like a quirk.

With whispers of joy in the crisp evening air,
We'll build up the chaos, with love and with care.
From dancing on rooftops to singing out loud,
It's a jolly good time, let's make winter proud!

Hushed Hums Beneath the Luminous Skies

The jingle of socks slips down the floor,
As giggles and laughter echo some more.
A cat in a hat, looking quite bemused,
Chasing shadows by the tree, thoroughly confused.

Hot cocoa spills while kids dance around,
With marshmallows flying, sweet chaos abound.
Snowflakes fall gently, covering the mess,
But who needs a broom? It's a holiday fest!

Flickering Dreams on Silver Snow

Snowmen wobble with carrot noses askew,
While penguins play tag, with a snowball or two.
A two-headed snowman, oh what a sight,
One hat says 'party' and the other 'goodnight'.

As sleds zip by with a thunderous cheer,
The neighbors all shout, 'Get out of here!'
But laughter bounces against frosty trees,
Who knew winter could be such a tease?

Reveries of Light in the Heart of Chill

A squirrel on skis is a sight to behold,
He flips and he flops, a legend unfolds.
With nut-filled pockets, he dashes in glee,
Past ice-covered branches, shouting, 'Look at me!'

The lights on the house blink rhythm and rhyme,
As cousins in onesies keep falling in time.
With cocoa mustaches and snowflake ears,
They toast to this season, full of good cheers.

Chilling Chimes and Warming Ties

The doorbell rings with a jingle galore,
Grandpa arrives, wearing socks on the floor.
He brings out the cookies, and to our surprise,
They're not cookies at all, just re-gifted pies!

Stumbling and tumbling, the kids start to fight,
Who gets the last gingerbread man in their sight?
The laughter erupts, as they jump with delight,
In a quest for sweet treasures, until the night.

Chimes of Frosted Dreams

The snowman wobbled, gave a spin,
With a carrot nose and a silly grin.
In the frosty air, laughter flies,
While penguins slide with comical cries.

Hot cocoa spills on a fuzzy sock,
As marshmallow snowmen take stock.
With every chime, the giggles grow,
In this frosted world, joy steals the show.

The Whispering Snowfall

Snowflakes whisper secrets low,
Like silly stories no one would know.
The cat in the hat is planning a dance,
While dogs grab snowballs and act like a prance.

Chasing their tails, round and round,
They create a chorus of pitter-patter sound.
With each soft flake, the giggles ignite,
In a winter wonderland, oh what a sight!

Echoes of a Silver Eve

Tinsel tangled in a festive mess,
Santa's list is a guessing test.
Elves on ladders, hats askew,
They sing carols that sound like goo.

Cookies left out, a whole buffet,
Santa may munch, then roll away.
The echoes of cheer bounce off each wall,
As feisty gnomes prepare for the ball.

Hues of Yuletide Glow

The lights twinkle as cats chase balls,
While gingerbread men make daring calls.
With gumdrop buttons and icing galore,
They sneak around, then tumble and score.

The fireplace pops with a merry crack,
While socks hang on the door with a whack.
In the jovial air, laughter does flow,
Amidst the frolic of colors that glow.

A Reverie Bright on a Pillowed Night

In dreams of sugar plums, I tread,

Hopping on socks, then falling in bed.

The cat is plotting a nibble or two,

As visions dance in the light of the moon.

With cocoa spilling, a marshmallow dive,

Hot chocolate rivers where giggles arrive.

Snowflakes are sneezes; oh what a sight,

The dog in a sweater? He put up a fight!

Frosty Whispers and Fiery Hearts

A snowman struts with a carrot-nosed grin,
Waving to neighbors, where do I begin?
He's got a top hat, and a smile so wide,
But I fear for the dog, let's not put him outside!

The tree is aglow with lights all around,
Tinsel that sparkles as laughter resounds.
Grandma's baking cookies; I sneak just a bite,
She catches me grinning, oh, what a delight!

Shimmering Hues in the Darkening Skies

Fa-la-la-la, the carolers sing,

While I trip over my own winter fling.

My scarf is too long, I'm tangled, oh dear,

As friends all erupt into giggles and cheer.

Outside in the chill, hot cider is shared,

With whispers of mischief, nobody cared.

Fingers are freezing, faces aglow,

But hot soup awaits; now that's how we roll!

Embers Awaiting the Arrival of the Frost

By the fire, we gather, a marshmallow fight,
S'mores turn to chaos; oh, what a sight!
The cat in the corner looks quite bemused,
While we laugh and joke, our timing confused.

Outside the snowflakes begin to accrue,
Looks like that snowman's not built for a crew.
With mittens and laughter, we tumble and fall,
The dogs are delighted—oh, what a free-for-all!

The Promise of Warmth in the Cold

When the frost bites, and snowflakes play,
My cat steals the blanket, what can I say?
Hot cocoa's a friend, with marshmallows galore,
Yet my socks are mismatched, oh what a chore!

The neighbors are grinning, their lights all aglow,
While my bulbs flicker like a circus show.
We dance through the ice, on ungrateful feet,
And laugh till we stumble on the frosty street.

Crystal Chords Amidst the Silence

Snowmen are grinning, with noses of coal,
While I'm stuck inside, losing track of my goal.
The music that jingles comes straight from the fridge,
My attempts at a song sound like a sad bridge.

Icicles sparkle, hang like tiny spears,
As I try to explain my holiday cheers.
The cookies I baked, oh boy, what a sight,
They're more like a science project, with fright!

Harmony of Lights in Icy Stillness

The carolers sing, but I'm out of tune,
My voice seems to shiver like the cold afternoon.
With mittens on hands and a hat on my head,
I tripped on the ice, and now I'm seeing red!

Dancing 'round the tree, oh what a delight,
'Til my uncle starts twirling, and it's pure fright.
We laugh and we giggle, exchanging our cheer,
As we swap silly stories that brighten the year.

Dreams Adrift on a Snowy Canvas

Snowflakes are whispering secrets to me,
While I'm busy searching for a lost cup of tea.
The sledding looks tempting, but I might just fall,
If I take one more step, I'll make a snowball.

Through windows we watch, the snowflakes parade,
While I'm stuck in the kitchen, extracting a braid.
The laughter outside, how I long to partake,
But I'm too busy feasting on grandma's cake!

Elysian Dreams Amidst the Snowfall

In the frosty air, the penguins glide, They wear tiny hats, with feathers dyed. Snowflakes giggle as they start to twirl, Even the trees seem to dance and whirl.

A snowman winks with a carrot nose, While squirrels sled down, striking a pose. Hot cocoa spills on my fluffy hat, I sip too quick and, oh! What of that?

The ice skates clash, a comical roar, As my friend spins and then hits the floor. We laugh so hard, it's a jolly sight, In this winter wonder, all fun feels right.

As night falls down with stars a-glow, We plan a snowball fight, a fierce show. With laughter ringing in the chilly night, Our playful spirits take wondrous flight.

The Sweet Resonance of Winter's Kiss

Jingle bells jangle, with a twist and twirl, The reindeer are prancing, their tails in a whirl. One stole my hat, now he's on the run, Chasing him down is sheer winter fun!

Frosty the dude, with his hat now askew, Claims he's a surfer, riding waves made of dew. The penguins cry, and the owls roll their eyes, As snowflakes chuckle under starlit skies.

We build a tall tower of snow and of ice, It topples like laughter, oh, isn't it nice? The snowflakes giggle, with each snowy fall, While we dodge and weave in this frosty brawl.

Hot cider is spilled, but we drink it with glee, A toast to the laughter that sets winter free. With jingles and jests, the cold we embrace, In this whimsical season, joy takes its place.

Melodies Beneath the Snow

Jingle jangle in the street,
Snowflakes dance on furry feet.
Carrots grin on snowmen's face,
While penguins waddle, strut with grace.

Hot cocoa spills, oh what a sight,
Marshmallows float like clouds in flight.
Sleds go zooming, laughter's bright,
As snowflakes swirl in pure delight.

Reindeer games in icy glow,
Can't catch them, they're fast, you know!
Santa's hat is stuck on high,
He just can't reach it—oh my, my!

Chimneys puffing, smoke like cheer,
Bunnies hop, they've lost all fear.
A snowball fight, all for one,
'Til someone slips and ends the fun!

Twinkling Candles in the Dark

Candles flicker, shadows sway,
Gingerbread men have come to play.
Mittens mismatched on the floor,
While cats are plotting, wanting more.

Hot spice scents twist and entwine,
Neighbors' carols sound divine.
A rooftop squirrel—oh, what a view!
He's jamming hard, just like a crew!

Nuts are roasting, got to share,
But someone spilled them everywhere!
Giggles float on winter air,
As cupcakes tumble down the stair.

Wish you could join the festive spree,
With twinkling lights and jubilee.
Candles blink, it's all a blur,
Join in quick—don't be demure!

Frostbitten Lullabies

Stars shiver softly overhead,
While snowmen snore in silvery bed.
Frosty whispers, dreams take flight,
As polar bears dance late at night.

Chilly winds sing a tune bizarre,
Gummy bears in a snowy car.
Slippers squeak on icy floors,
As moonbeams slide through open doors.

Hot biscuits pop, 'how do you do?',
While mice play chess with brew in view.
Pine cones jam in a merry band,
Creating chaos—oh, how they stand!

When morning breaks with creamy hues,
Let's toast to joy and winter snooze.
With laughter ringing all around,
What a day to be snowbound!

Radiance in the Chill

Bright lights twinkle from every eave,
While kids believe in magic, believe!
A frosty dog with a shiny nose,
Chasing down candy that giggles and grows.

Puzzles crunch underneath each step,
As puppies sneak in more than a pep.
Frozen noses, red-hot cheeks,
And snowflakes tickle as each one peaks.

Sleds collide with a boom and a bang,
As laughter erupts with a giggling clang.
In the hush of dusk, the fun is still,
Who knew cold could give such a thrill?

Elves baking cookies, what a delight,
With sprinkles flying, like stars in flight.
So let's toast to all in glee,
For winter's magic, fun, and spree!

Illuminations of the Heart on Frigid Nights

In snowflakes' waltz, my nose turns red,
As I sip my cocoa, dreaming in bed.
My socks are mismatched, but who would care?
Laughter wraps around like a fluffy chair.

A cat on a window, plotting my fate,
While outside, the tow truck is sticking in late.
The neighbor's lights flash, a wild disco ball,
As I dodge stray snowballs with a comical fall.

Stars Sing Songs of Winter's Grace

The stars above twinkle, a sight so sweet,
While I trip on the sidewalk, give winter a greet.
My scarf's in a twist, like a child's poor toy,
But inside I'm giggling, embracing the joy.

Frosty windows tell tales of mirth and glee,
While snowmen play chess with a squirrel and me.
A snowball fight starts, oh what a tease,
As I duck and I weave, barely escape with ease.

Cozy Realms within Twinkling Light

The lights on the tree flicker and fade,
As I dance through the kitchen, snack choices made.
My mom shoots me looks, with an eye roll and sigh,
But my cookie dough smile could light up the sky.

Hot tea in my mug, with a splash of delight,
As I trip on my cat, still hiding from light.
The stockings are hung by the chimney with flair,
But one's on the floor, thanks to kitty's dare.

Anthems of Love in a Frosty Realm

The snow is a blanket, so crisp and so bright,
But my ears are so cold, they give me a fright.
With mittens oversized, I wave to the moon,
While my socks get all soggy, oh crude costume!

Caroling tunes echo through frosty air,
As I serenade squirrels, with a comb for flair.
A snowman nods back, his face made of ice,
We'll share a chuckle; not once, not twice.

Twilight Whispers of Farewell

In the glow of fading light,
A penguin slips, what a sight!
Sliding down the snowy hill,
Laughing still, oh what a thrill.

Frosty noses, cheeks so red,
Duck in snow, oh what a spread!
Carrots lost and hats askew,
A snowman grins and winks at you.

Tinsel tangled in the tree,
A cat leaps, oh let it be!
With ribbons flying through the air,
Every corner, holiday flair!

In winter's chill, we find the fun,
With each mishap, we come undone!
Laughter echoes through the night,
Bring on more, oh, what a sight!

Harmony in the Hushed Night

Caroling cats in a snowy fest,
Chasing lights, they are the best!
With paws that pounce and eyes that gleam,
Join the laughter, what a dream!

Furry friends all lined in rows,
Jumping high, where nobody goes!
Sledding down with yips and yowls,
Who knew winter brought such howls?

Twinkling lights on every house,
While squirrels plot with stealthy grouse.
A hoot from afar, a giggle near,
This winter time, filled with cheer!

Mittens lost and scarves a mess,
Gingerbread men in a bold dress!
As laughter spreads, we gather round,
In festive fun, true joy is found!

Shimmering Wonders of the Season

Twinkling stars dance in the sky,
While snowflakes twirl and flit on by.
A reindeer slips and bumps a tree,
What chaos, oh how could this be?

Mittens flying, children chase,
A snowball hits right in the face!
Frosty breath in evening chill,
Howling laughter, what a thrill!

Charming lights strung up with flair,
Someone's tangled in a snare.
Jingle bells that go 'ding-dong',
Join the noise,come sing along!

Gifts that rattle, what's inside?
A puppy leaps, a fidgeting ride!
With joy that sparkles, shines so bright,
Embrace the laughter of the night!

Aglow with Hope and Cheer

Frosty nights and beaconed sights,
Giggling friends and snowball fights.
A silly hat on Grandpa's head,
Fluffy snowflakes in his bread!

Giggles echo, joy abounds,
With every whoosh, laughter sounds.
Puppies trot with wagging tails,
Chasing lights, leaving happy trails!

In the kitchen, cookies fly,
Sticky fingers, oh my, oh my!
Frosting swirls on noses bright,
What a merry, silly sight!

As daylight dims and shadows creep,
We toast our cheer before we sleep.
With giggles shared and stories spun,
This jolly time is just begun!

Celestial Ornaments Above

Sprinkled stars and jingle chimes,
The sky's a stage for silly crimes.
Socks on the line, they wave hello,
To lost mittens in the snow below.

Charming lights that blink and dance,
Last year's fruitcake took a chance.
It wobbles over, no one's quite bold,
To take a bite, it's 90 years old!

Giggling snowmen, buttons askew,
Wishing for noses that don't come unglued.
A snowball fight, a snow angel's glee,
As laughter rings from tree to tree.

Giggles rise with every bell,
Echoing throughout the chilly swell.
We're wrapped in joy, let spirits soar,
While the neighbor's cat hides behind the door.

Snowflakes and Secret Wishes

Whirling flakes, a frosty blizzard,
Snowmen gossip, can't get any lither.
They wear hats made of pot and old shoes,
While squirrels plot under winter's muse.

Hot cocoa spills, a slippery fate,
Mugs in hand, we laugh and debate.
Should marshmallows float like a cloud?
Or sink like my cat, who's feeling too proud?

Chasing dreams on sleds we ride,
Zooming down hills with laughter and pride.
Falling in snow, we're covered like cake,
Hopes for the day, our hearts will awake.

Giggles bubble with every wish,
Fingers crossed for an eggnog swish.
Carrots for noses scattered around,
While elves do backflips, look at them bound!

A Tapestry of Light and Ice

Twinkling strands on trees set high,
Glow like disco balls in the sky.
Underneath, the cookies melt,
A dog's in the kitchen, roof tiles he's dealt!

Icicles hang like nature's bling,
While birds ask, "What's that strange ringing?"
Carolers shout in offbeat tone,
As penguins slide right past their throne.

Plates piled high, it's feast or starve,
Last year's leftovers, none will brave.
Who's grandpa's hat? A family prize,
Being worn by auntie with gleeful eyes.

A burst of laughter in frosty air,
Joking about that great unicorn heir.
In this chilly frolic, we all can see,
Winter's mischief, that's pure glee!

Moments Wrapped in Time

Under blankets, we sip warm tea,
Sharing tales of glee with glee.
A tangle of lights and tangled hair,
Uncle Fred dances without a care.

Wrapping paper flies, a colorful mess,
Surprises inside, we all guess.
Who's got the socks, who has the pride?
While the cat steals gifts, oh how it glides!

Tick-tock laughter as we countdown,
Merry chaos in this merry town.
Frozen pizza, more than a crime,
We raise a toast to happy times.

Old photos shared, memories vast,
Funny faces from the past.
Time wraps around in playful rhyme,
Leaving smiles that forever chime.

Serenade of the Season

The snowflakes dive, just like my cat,
She plops down, wearing my old hat.
With every twirl, she makes a mess,
Is this a pet or just my stress?

The roof's a stage for squirrels that leap,
In their furry coats, they'll never sleep.
They chitter and chatter, what a fun sight,
I witness their antics through the night.

The cocoa spills, the marshmallows stray,
My mug's a canoe afloat in the fray.
As laughter echoes, I burst into cheer,
Who knew winter could be so full of fear?

The lights on the tree are a tangled quest,
It's like giving my patience a funny test.
But in the end, as I sip and smile,
I find joy in chaos all the while.

Glistening Nights and Warm Fires

The socks mismatched, oh what a sight,
Worn proudly, I prance through the nightly light.
The flames crackle soft, the stories unfold,
Who knew my grandpa was ever so bold?

The neighbors carol, off-key and loud,
Each note they sing draws quite the crowd.
With bells that jingle, they stumble and sway,
I can't help but laugh at their festive display.

Outside the window, the icicles hang,
Like little spears, they're ready to clang.
A snowman smiles with a lopsided grin,
Guess he's had too much of the gin.

With cookies burnt and icing askew,
I'll take a bite, why not, it's true.
As laughter bounces, I'll raise my glass,
To nights adorned with joy, let time pass!

The Jingle of Heartfelt Greetings

With a grin so wide, I hang up the lights,
It's harder than it seems, even with all my might.
Last year's wreath has seen better days,
But it sparkles like disco in unpredictable ways.

The carols rumble, a bit off-tune,
Only my dog seems to join as a croon.
His howls blend nicely with the jingling bells,
Might make a hit, who knows? Only time tells.

The cookies stacked high, they lean and they sway,
One meatball slipped, took the sweets on a play.
As I chase sugar down, I trip on the rug,
Oh how I laugh, thanks to this holiday bug!

The gifts piled up, all wrapped with flair,
Who knows what's inside? A cat in despair?
With surprises galore, I can't help but cheer,
Let's hope the season's not full of sheer fear!

Shadows Dancing in the Moonlight

The snowman's hat keeps slipping away,
He blinks at me as if to say,
"I want a top hat, but hey, here's a cap!"
Well, this will do, let's create a flap!

The children sneak out for a playful fight,
Snowballs fly left, then dodge to the right.
A cheeky grin flashes 'til someone falls,
As laughter erupts, it echoing calls.

The moon chuckles down, silvering the night,
It sees the mischief and beams with delight.
From snow to giggles, the scene's gone awry,
Who knew winter plays had a sly alibi?

Beneath twinkling stars and whispers of fun,
In a world filled with joy, we all come undone.
With hearts so light, let's dance till we tire,
For life's little quirks always spark our fire!

Nocturne of the Snowbound Heart

The snowflakes swirl, a frosty dance,
Hot cocoa spills, oh what a chance!
The cat in winter, on the ledge,
Tries to catch snowflakes—what a hedge!

A squirrel in boots, so bold and spry,
Stashes acorns—oh my, oh my!
The doorbell rings, a snowy frost,
Who's out there? Oh dear, we're lost!

With mittens mismatched, we venture out,
A snowball fight—let's hear that shout!
But wait, my nose has turned a shade,
Into a snowman! No help is made!

Laughter erupts, a joyful cheer,
As we dive in, free of any fear.
Who knew the cold could bring such glee?
Except the snowman—oh, not me!

Frosted Serenade at Dusk

The trees wear coats, all white and bright,
Pinecone hats, oh what a sight!
Bunnies hop, in a snowy maze,
With tiny bells, they itch for praise!

The moon peeks out, a watchful eye,
As penguins slide, oh my, oh my!
Snowflakes tumble, in comical flight,
A dance of chaos, pure delight!

The snowman grins, a frosty beard,
But where's his nose? It disappears!
A carrot thief, oh what a game,
Who's to blame? The rabbit's to blame!

With laughter ringing, we sing a tune,
As hot chocolate simmers, in silver spoons.
Silly hats, and boots askew,
Winter wonder, no time to stew!

Candles Flicker, Shadows Dance

The candles sway, with a flickering glow,
Tiny shadows join, in a charming show.
A cat on the shelf, how it does prance,
Trying to catch every fleeting chance!

Gingerbread men begin to sway,
In a ballet where they can play.
Yet one finds out, with a panicked yelp,
That icing traps him—oh, what a help!

The cookies scatter, on the floor,
As kiddos munch, and ask for more.
With frosting crowns, they giggle and play,
While sugar rushes usher in the fray!

No chilly winds can freeze this fun,
As laughter echoes, hearts weigh a ton.
Our merry corner bright, not a frown,
With shadows dancing, let's twirl around!

Echoing Joy in Crystal Light

A jingle bell, a cat that sings,
Got lost amidst all shiny things.
With mismatched socks, we dance and spin,
Amidst the laughter, let fun begin!

The snowman rolls, a ball of fluff,
Wears a hat that's clearly too tough.
As children giggle, the sun shifts low,
Their cheeky boots leave tracks in the snow!

A snow angel flops, face-down in glee,
As cocoa spills—oh no, not me!
The mittens squabble, both colors clash,
Yet hearts unite in a joyful splash!

So raise a toast with mugs held high,
To snowy days that gently fly.
For though the chill bites at our nose,
In every heartbeat, true warmth grows!

Frosty Kisses Under the Mistletoe.

Snowflakes dancing in the breeze,
Socks are slipping, oh, with ease!
Hot cocoa spills, a funny sight,
We laugh and laugh 'til late at night.

Mittens tangled, yarns all stray,
A cat jumps high, oh what a play!
Face full of tinsel, stuck like glue,
Who knew festive could feel so skewed?

Chilly noses, rosy cheeks,
Catching snowflakes on our cheek peaks.
A mistletoe mishap, oh dear me,
You kissed my dog, not quite the key!

So here's to the giggles and playful cheer,
Our winter wonderland, filled with good beer.
With frostbitten laughter we all will toast,
To funny moments we love the most!

Jingle Echoes in Frosted Air

Sleigh bells ringing, oh what a sound,
Frosty feet dancing all around.
Tinsel tangled, dogs in a chase,
Hot chocolate mustache on every face!

Jingle hats flipped, we spin and whirl,
Snowmen wobble, what a funny twirl!
A mitten escapes, flies high in the sky,
Shouts of laughter as it passes by.

Bouncing around like a reindeer crew,
Slip on the ice, oh what did I do?
Frosty giggles fill the bright night,
Snowflakes flutter like pure delight.

Bells keep ringing without a care,
As laughter echoes in the frosted air.
Jiggly bellies from cookies we eat,
Our jolly mischief is hard to beat!

Whispers of Yuletide Glow

Under bright lights, we shimmy and shake,
Gingerbread men begin to quake.
A tip of the hat, a slip on the floor,
We tumble and giggle, can't take any more!

Whispers of mischief in every nook,
Caught in the act, a sneaky look.
Decorated cats, oh what a sight,
They wear our hats; oh, what a fright!

Frosty giggles all through the night,
With candy canes and pure delight.
A snowball fight gone wildly wrong,
Ends in laughter, our hearts belong.

Here's to the magic, the joy we make,
With every hiccup and every mistake.
The glow of the season, so bright and true,
Is only complete with laughter, too!

Chimes of the Frosty Eve

Echoing chimes ring out so clear,
Snowmen giggle; oh dear, oh dear!
With scarves wrapped tight, we prance about,
Falling face-first, we scream and shout!

Slippery sidewalks, a ballet of fun,
Twisting and turning, oh who's won?
Jolly old hats that fly on by,
Caught in a tree, oh my, oh my!

Hot cider spills, a splash on my toes,
Our laughter rings out while winter glows.
Merry mishaps, we can't contain,
The joy in our hearts, like snow, we can't feign!

So raise a glass to the frosty air,
In every blunder, we find a share.
The chimes will echo, and so will we,
For laughter's the gift, just wait and see!

Melodies Under Snowy Skies

Flakes like feathers swirl and twirl,
A snowman's hat begins to whirl!
My dog leaps high, a furry clown,
Paws flailing in the frozen gown.

Hot cocoa spills, a marshmallow dive,
Just like my uncle when he arrives!
Snowball fights turn into a mess,
He claims he won, I must confess.

Elves in stores with prices great,
Demanding gifts but why such weight?
A visit with Santa leads to dread,
He ate the cookies—he's too well fed!

So here we dance in chilly air,
With laughter loud, our moments rare.
The season's bright with silly cheer,
Each frosty breath carries glee near.

Radiance in the Silent Night

The lights outside blink left and right,
While cats plot pounces, oh what a sight!
A reindeer prances down the lane,
With kids outside, playing a game.

Old folks wrapped in blankets, oh my!
Snoring softly, dreams fly high.
I sneak a peek at their soft snores,
One catches me, and laughter roars!

The mistletoe hangs, an awkward stage,
Where Uncle Bob steps, oh what a rage!
He slips and slides, a comic show,
Kissing the floor, sharing his woe.

With carols sung in out-of-tune,
We raise a glass beneath the moon.
Cheers to fun, with giggles we say,
Readiness for mischief here to stay.

Twilight Twinkling on Icy Branches

Icicles glimmer, a sparkly fight,
As mittens disappear, oh what a sight!
Frosty the snowman takes a fall,
With carrot nose bouncing like a ball.

Sledding down hills, kids scream in glee,
While parents just hope it's not them you'll see!
Snowplow drivers smile, feeling bold,
But watch out! They're freezing, if not told!

Baking cookies, flour in the air,
My cat cleans up; she doesn't care.
Sprinkling sprinkles, a sugary mess,
The cookie monster claims success!

Light strings flicker like fireflies,
As laughter mixes with joyful cries.
In this chill, we're cozy and bright,
With stories told throughout the night.

Harmony of the Chill Breeze

Snowflakes dance like they own the street,
While toddlers tumble, oh what a feat!
Furry hats and mittens worn loud,
Pushing each other, claiming the crowd.

The goofiest sweaters gracing the hall,
With patterns that baffle, confusing us all.
Grandma's frozen pie, a sight to behold,
It's either pie or a reindeer, I'm told!

With every cheer, the warmth grows near,
Laughter blooms, banishing fear.
We hunt for mischief, with twinkling eyes,
Wrapped in warmth, under winter skies.

A Song of Hope Beneath the White Veil

Under a blanket, fluffy and bright,
We toss snowballs, what a sight!
The squirrel mocks us with a cheer,
While we trip and yelp, oh dear!

Hot cocoa spills, a festive mess,
Laughter sprouts, we still confess.
As hats fly off in wild delight,
We chase them down with all our might.

Snowmen wobble, noses askew,
They join our party, a crazy crew.
With carrot sticks and an old scarf,
They dance along, oh how we laugh!

Beneath the stars, our spirits soar,
In this winter's joke, we can't ignore.
With every slip and every fall,
We're just a bunch of giggling fools, after all.

Glowing Tales on the Crispest Nights

The moonlight glimmers on frozen streams,
As we tell stories, wild as dreams.
A sledder flies past, what a show!
We cheer him on while we freeze our toes.

Hot pies cooling, a pie fight soon!
Laughter erupts beneath the moon.
One hits the dog, he gives us a stare,
With whipped cream splatters in his hair.

Jingle hats wobble on folks we meet,
While we wiggle our noses to keep warm feet.
The reindeer parade takes quite a turn,
As one takes a leap with a daring churn!

With giggles echoing in frosty air,
We stumble home without a care.
In this cold embrace, friendships shine bright,
Spreading joy and warmth in every bite.

Echoes of Laughter Amidst Snowflakes

Snowflakes tumble like lost balloon,
We chase after them, like playful raccoons.
With every catch, we dance and scream,
Life's a comedy, or so it seems!

Puddle splashes send us all shrieking,
The laughter echoes, joyous and sneaking.
With every sip of hot marshmallow,
Our giggles burst like a cheerful yellows.

Gnarled trees wear their coats of white,
While we turn cartwheels, what a sight!
A tumble over, a tumble back,
We get up laughing, no sign of slack.

As the day fades, we light up the flares,
Our silliness twinkling, with reckless stares.
From ice skating slips to riotous cheer,
This joyful season reigns all year.

Mirthful Nights and Brisk Breezes

With frosty whiskers and rosy cheeks,
We huddle together, this warmth we seek.
As chimneys puff like dragons of old,
We laugh at the wonders that never get told.

Mittens mismatched, oh what a sight!
We wander deeper into the night.
With tinsel in hair and sparkles galore,
Our laughter carries to every door.

Hot soup spills as we hear the call,
Of snowball fights, we must have it all.
With silly hats and tangled scarves,
We're here to shine, like bright-eyed stars.

In the warmth of our quirky nest,
We find that silly is truly the best.
With giggles ringing through icy air,
We spread our joy everywhere!

Tidings of Warmth in Bitter Winds

When frosty winds begin to blow,
We bundle up in layers, you know.
Hot cocoa spills on mittens tight,
As snowflakes dance in silly flight.

The snowman winks with a carrot nose,
Wearing my scarf, all frayed and froze.
He gives a wave to passersby,
While I just laugh and wonder why.

Sledding down hills on a pancake flat,
I scream, "Watch out!" but it's just a cat.
With giggles rising through the cold air,
We crash and tumble—oh, what a scare!

Yet warmth surrounds with friends so dear,
In jolly sweaters that bring us cheer.
Together we share tales and treats,
As laughter echoes, oh, what feats!

A Tapestry of Glistening Dreams

In the corner, a tree stands tall,
With lights that twinkle and ornaments small.
A cat appears, with a leap and bound,
To swat at baubles all around.

Pine-scented air and cookies galore,
We bake till we can't fit through the door.
Flour flies, and a whisk goes rogue,
Making us all out to be a jesting vogue.

With jingles and jangles, the doorbell rings,
Neighbors come 'round for the joy it brings.
We swap the gifts that might be a flop,
I got a lamp that will never stop!

As laughter fills up the frosty night,
We toast to moments of pure delight.
Creating memories, and jokes that gleam,
In this dazzling net of a whimsical dream!

Glistening Tranquility Under Starlit Nights

Under skies where the chilly stars twinkle,
The ground is crisp, and the air's a sprinkle.
With snowflakes kicking up our feet,
Every step's a silly little treat.

We build a fort from icy walls,
With marshmallow fights, oh how it calls!
A snowball flings with a comical splash,
I duck and cover. Oh! What a crash!

The sleds glide down, oh what delight,
But who biffs it first? Oh, what a sight!
We tumble and roll, like bears in a den,
And laugh till we cry—let's do it again!

Then huddled together, hot cocoa in hand,
We recount our follies—oh, isn't it grand?
With starlit giggles echoing true,
We relish the charm that this night'll imbue.

Lullabies in the Stillness of Snow

Quiet nights when the world turns white,
Snow blankets everything, such a sight.
While echoes of laughter from friends we chase,
There's magic and mischief in this frozen space.

We crawl in the snow, making angels divine,
Only to find, along comes a line!
A pup with a wag and a curious quest,
Darts through our art, oh, that little pest!

With mittens mismatched and noses red,
We tell ghost stories beneath the spread.
Whispers of wonder, they fill the air,
Like sugar plums dancing—a whimsical flare.

So here in the stillness, we find our fun,
With memories spun like the threads we've run.
In the lullabies of night's soft glow,
We capture joy in the dance of the snow!

Glimmers of Joy in a Winter Wonderland

Snowflakes dance like little ants,
While mittens start their funny prance.
Hot cocoa spills in clumsy fumbles,
As laughter lifts the chilly tumbles.

Sleds zoom past like racing cars,
With snowman heads and carrot stars.
Each slip and slide brings giggles bright,
In a world low on winter bite.

Chasing puppies through the drifts,
They leap and bound with frosty shifts.
We all wear hats that fall askew,
Oh, the sights that we pursue!

In snowball fights, we throw and duck,
With cheeks that glow, we tempt our luck.
By night's warm fire, we share a cheer,
As silly tales just seem to clear.

Frost-kissed Fantasies Under the Moon

With tinsel traps and sparkly wands,
We weave our dreams and make silly plans.
Glistening snowflakes catch our breath,
As we dance like penguins, mocking death.

Hot cider spills on frosty paws,
With gales that echo laugh-filled flaws.
Through twinkling lights, our shadows sway,
As squirrels giggle in a playful fray.

Snowmen grin with buttons askew,
Somehow wearing a hat that's my shoe!
Beneath the stars, we sing off-key,
But no one cares; we're feeling free.

In this chilly whimsy, hearts are bright,
While snowflakes twinkle in the night.
Oh, how we frolic, jump, and tease,
Making memories with winter's breeze.

The Soft Glow of Evening Flurries

Under the streetlight's gentle beam,
We toss our hats with reckless gleam.
While twirling round till we get dizzy,
Our noses melt, oh so frizzy!

As flakes begin to cover ground,
We chuckle soft, a merry sound.
The frosty air is a playful friend,
As giggles bubble and never end.

Snow forts rise like castles tall,
With epic battles, we're bound to fall.
But rolling down in soft, white fluff,
Brings laughter loud, this fun's enough!

With cups of cheer to warm our hands,
We toast to friends and snowy lands.
As night drifts in, the moonlight glows,
While shivering, joy is all we chose.

Echoed Laughter on Snowy Paths

Stumbling through the drifts so deep,
We trip and fall, yet never weep.
Our footprints dance like silly ghosts,
Each laugh we share, each joy we boast.

Through the crunch of frost beneath our shoes,
We launch our jokes like little clues.
Hot soup spills from our frozen cups,
While snowball dodgers make us pups!

Beneath spun lights, we twirl and spin,
Finding laughter where we begin.
The chilly winds may chill our toes,
Yet warmth arises when humor flows.

So here we stand, hearts intertwined,
In a snowy maze, our spirits aligned.
With echoes ringing through the night,
We savor joy, and winter's light.

Glowing Hearts in the Frosty Air

In the chilly breeze, snowmen wear grins,
Their carrot noses point where mischief begins.
With frosted eyebrows and scarves of bright red,
They dance in the moonlight, while I sip my bread.

Chubby cheeks glow as laughter rings loud,
Snowball fights break out in the teeming crowd.
But watch where you throw; there's a sneaky cat,
Who dodges and ducks—what a cheeky brat!

Snowflakes twirl down, like confetti from skies,
Hot cocoa spills forth from mugs set on pies.
Lips turn to icicles, noses a shade blue,
While we stumble away from a slippery cue.

So here's to the winter, so jolly and bright,
Where giggles are echoes, and time takes flight.
We'll stomp in the puddles, we'll slide 'til we fall,
In glowing hearts' laughter, we rejoice in it all.

Frosty Kisses Beneath Twilight Skies

Twilight whispers secrets to the winking stars,
While pigeons in hats are dreaming of cars.
There's a chill in the air, or is that just me?
The squirrels are plotting, oh, what could it be?

Frosty kisses, oh what a sight to behold,
A penguin with snowshoes is bartering gold.
While kids on the swing set are flying so high,
Attracting the seagulls—oh, what a sly guy!

The snowflakes are doing a wiggly dance,
As hot dogs in sweaters get caught in a trance.
With mittens too small, and scarves way too long,
We jingle and tangle, all happy and wrong.

So toast to our antics, absurd as they seem,
With toasty warm marshmallows, every dream's gleam.
We wobble and giggle till frostbite's our fate,
In frosty kisses, we seal love's great slate.

The Magic of Light in a Wintry Landscape

Snowflakes glimmer softly, like fairy lights bright,
As my cat weaves through snowdrifts with new-found delight.
A reindeer on roller skates whirls with a grin,
While I chase after shadows, my patience wears thin.

The moon plays peek-a-boo with old-fashioned trees,
As carolers serenade the passing warm breeze.
There's laughter and whimsy in every warm heart,
As snowmen hold hands, in their fragile art.

Frosted windows tell tales of jesters and more,
Each twinkle of magic captures tales we adore.
But beware of the dog who's plotting a feast,
With crumbs from the table, he's ready to beast!

In lights all aglow, we sip cider with cheer,
While snowflakes dance closer, whispering near.
So let's trim the tree with the most silly lights,
In the magic of laughter on long winter nights.

Tranquil Nights Wrapped in White Veils

A blanket of snow drapes the world in white,
While giggles of children echo through the night.
Sleds fly down hills, like birds on a spree,
While I watch from the corner, sipping my tea.

The stars glitter down on precarious roofs,
As penguins swap recipes—oh, the goofs!
With snowmen inspecting their carrot-stick hats,
While I ponder why igloos can't house those cats.

In tranquil enchantment, the world holds its breath,
While the chill in the air brings the freshest of zest.
Frosty toes twitch while we prance to and fro,
As snowflakes remind me that winter's for show.

So let's raise a toast as we giggle and glide,
With snowflakes that twinkle, and warmth as our guide.
Wrapped snug in the humor this night has revealed,
In tranquil delight, our joy is unsealed.

A Symphony of Embered Hearts

In layers thick, we waddle fast,
A snowman's grin, his nose a blast.
Carrots stolen from the fridge,
A snowy sight, we can't out-ridge.

Laughter echoes, a sledding fall,
With every slip, we hear the call.
Hot cocoa spills, a marshmallow fight,
Who knew that snow could bring such light?

Frosty flakes, they dance and twirl,
In mittens lost, our fingers curl.
We race the wind with giggles loud,
As if we're kings, this snow, our crowd.

As dusk arrives, the lights appear,
We think they shine just for us, dear.
With each soft wink, the stars conspire,
To match our glee, set hearts on fire.

Sledding Through Twinkling Stars

We strap our boots, it's time to zoom,
On wooden sleds, out in the gloom.
With cheeks so red and noses blue,
We slide on ice, just me and you.

A tumble here, a tumble there,
Now tangled up in frosty air.
We chase our hats as they take flight,
With whoops and hollers, what a sight!

The trees wear coats of glistening white,
As snowflakes whirl, oh what a night!
With every glide, we laugh with glee,
In winter's grasp, we're wild and free.

Underneath the twinkling sky,
We'll toast marshmallows, oh me, oh my!
With every bite and sugary cheer,
These swirling dreams we hold so dear.

The Glow of Hearthside Tales

Around the fire, tales do flow,
With socks so thick, we steal the show.
Grandpa's yarns, they twist and wind,
As cookies crumble, memories bind.

Hot cider bubbles, a spicy tease,
While kittens pounce on snowy knees.
With goofy hats and laughter bright,
We share our dreams into the night.

The flames flicker like cheeky sprites,
We roast our laughs, with goofy bites.
Old stories sung, the silly, the wise,
Each chuckle shared, the best surprise!

As daylight wanes and shadows play,
We sip and share till break of day.
Together here, we find our cheer,
In flickering lights, winter's dear.

Slices of Joy in Frosted Air

With peppermints and ginger snaps,
We gather 'round, the laughter claps.
Each riddle tossed, it flies like snow,
In festive cheer, where joy can grow.

The cake is big, the icing sticks,
Watch out for crumbs, oh what a mix!
In every bite, a sweet delight,
We giggle and bounce, hearts feel so light.

With scarves pulled tight and noses red,
We share our dreams, and dreams we spread.
In frosted air, we slice the night,
With joy and glee, oh what a sight!

As snowflakes fall like happy tears,
We toast our hopes and face our fears.
In every laugh, a story spun,
Our hearts unite, the warmth of fun.

A Journey Through Chill and Warmth

Socks on the tree, oh what a sight,
They wiggle and jingle, it feels just right.
Hot cocoa spills on my cozy chair,
As marshmallows ride, a turbulent air.

Snowflakes are falling, they dance, oh so sly,
While I chase them down, like kids, oh my!
My nose is a beacon, so red it glows,
As icicles drip with mischievous throes.

Grandpa's snoring tunes, a festive hum,
As we plan a feast and then all go numb.
The cat on the table, what's this? A feast!
He pounces on crumbs; oh, the fun never ceased!

In mittens and hats, we venture outside,
Yet trip on our feet, oh, how we glide!
Laughter erupts in this wintery spree,
Fashionable fumbles are quite the decree!

Holiday Whispers in Icy Echoes

Snowmen stand guard, a frosty brigade,
Their carrot-nose tales, a veggie charade.
I twirl with delight on the slippery lane,
Then land with a thud, oh what a pain!

The grandpa in gifts, a bearded old chap,
Rummages through boxes, ready to unwrap.
But boxes unite in a paper-filled fight,
As cousins all giggle, oh what a sight!

Rooms filled with laughter, a cacophony sweet,
As dogs chase the kids on their tiny little feet.
A game of charades, we fumble and jest,
With half-hearted guesses, we laugh at the best.

The food piled high, yet we play 'taste test',
With pies that have lost every possible zest.
Yet each silly moment, we hold dear tonight,
As snowflakes keep falling, we bask in the light.

Kindling Light in the Midst of Haze

Candles are flickering, the glowing parade,
While cats plot mischief, a shadowy charade.
With eggnog in hand, and a twist of the lime,
We toast to the times, quite silly and prime!

A tree dressed in tinsel, bright lights blinking fast,
Yet one cheeky bulb just won't hold on fast.
We laugh at the stories, of mishaps and thrills,
Like grandma's false teeth that slide down the hills!

Puppies and kittens, they chase and collide,
With ribbons and bows, oh what a grand ride!
Together we grin, as hot soup goes cold,
In moments like these, the best tales unfold.

So gather 'round close, with hugs that embrace,
As laughter erupts in this whimsical space.
A toast to the chaos, the joy, and the cheer,
For in all the laughter, the warmth draws us near.

Winter's Embrace Beneath Glittering Stars

Stars twinkle brightly, a scattered delight,
While snowmen hold truths, their secrets at night.
A snowball's a weapon, a playful attack,
And just when you launch, you'll find you're whacked!

The puppy runs wild, a monster of fluff,
As we try to catch him, it's quite the tough stuff.
With mittens mismatched, we stumble and trip,
As laughter erupts with each planned little slip!

Hot cakes taste better with way too much cream,
As we laugh and we bake, all caught in a dream.
A scarf now a blanket, a fashion faux pas,
With chairs all a-tilt, we raise a loud "hurrah!"

So dance in the snow with your heart full of glee,
For moments of joy are forever the key.
In sparkles and giggles, in warmth and in cheer,
We'll laugh with abandon, for laughter's a dear!

Milton Keynes UK
Ingram Content Group UK Ltd.
UKHW022341171124
451242UK00007B/78